A Common Sense for Parish Life

Liturgy Training Publications

This project was coordinated by Robert Piercy for
Liturgy Training Publications and Tabor Publishing.
Those who participated in the discussions that led to
this book are:

> Eileen Anderson
> Paul Covino
> Catherine Dooley, OP
> Timothy Fitzgerald
> Ralph Fletcher
> Gabe Huck
> Jane Marie Osterholt, OSF
> Robert Piercy
> Jo Rotunno
> John Wright

Editor: Gabe Huck
Production editor: Deborah Bogaert
Design: M. Urgo
Typesetting: Karen Mitchell
Printed by Original Smith Printing of Bloomington,
Illinois.

Copublished with Tabor Publishing.

Library of Congress Cataloging-in-Publications Data
Huck, Gabe.
   A common sense for parish life / Gabe Huck.
     p.   cm.
   1. Pastoral theology — Catholic Church.
   2. Catholic Church — United States — Liturgy.
   3. Catechetics — Catholic Church.   4. Parishes —
United States.   I. Title.
   BX1913.H83   1996   95-46978
   253' .08' 822 — dc20   CIP

ISBN 1-56854-145-7
SENSE

9.00

3-2-99

Contents

INTRODUCTION

Through decades of difficult work in the first half of the twentieth century, the movements within the Roman Catholic church for the renewal of liturgy, catechesis and social justice grew together. They were not even three separate movements but often the same people with their same convictions working on different aspects of the same challenge. These movements climaxed in the Second Vatican Council. The work that already had been done served as the prologue to the great documents written there and supplemented in the years that followed.

But all has not been well. We have often tried to put the vision of the Council into bureaucratic and corporate structures where it is not at home. We have specialized: Those who work in liturgy talk only to those who work in liturgy. Religious educators have their own meetings and make jokes about the liturgy folks. Those in social concern can't understand why any priority in these desperate and violent times should be given to the luxuries of liturgy and catechesis. We have developed different vocabularies as well as different assumptions about the church. This is not helpful in a time when those who would like to forget Vatican II altogether are sitting in places of power.

This book comes from one effort to regain and renew the unity of liturgy, catechesis and the doing of justice. The principles enunciated and commented on here come from discussions among various people associated with Liturgy Training

Publications of Chicago, Illinois, and Tabor Publishing of Allen, Texas. These discussions themselves revealed to us the lack of common ground.

We thought it would be helpful to people in parish and diocesan work if we wrote down the points on which we came to agreement and suggested that these might be a starting point for pastoral discussion. What we suggest is something as simple as a parish staff or parish council giving over half an hour of their regular meeting to reading and discussing these points one by one.

Even those parishes recognized as somehow "successful," whether large or small, may need such an examination to see if their success is more in the model of corporate America than in that of the gospel and its assembly. And every parish can rejoice if its leadership takes the time to ponder the unspoken assumptions that foster or hinder the gospel. For many, it will be a new experience to struggle with those underpinnings. As Woody Guthrie would tell us, "Take it easy, but take it."

We have structured this book to slow down and deepen the discussion. Thus, the principles should not be grouped but should be considered one at a time. And anyone participating in the discussion should know: Preparation is presumed.

The first two pages of each principle are not for the group to work on together but are for each individual to work on before meeting for discussion. On these two pages, the same questions and exercises are given for each principle. Some will appeal, some will not. But at least a few of them should engage each participant so that when the group does meet, everyone participating will bring the notes they have made. The discussion begins, then, with a sharing of some of these notes.

Why such stress on preparation? Because each of us needs time and some method to draw out of our own hearts and minds insights that will prove useful to the community. We believe it is vital that participants commit themselves to this individual preparation before engaging in discussion.

At the discussion itself, let the four questions on the third page of each principle be a guide. You may well evolve other, more appropriate questions. Again, use the space in this book: Fill it with notes. The final part of dealing with each principle will lead you to the last pages of this book. Become familiar with pages 46, 47 and 48 from the very start of your work. Remember that the goal is not a new program but a new and shared understanding of how a parish lives and works. That understanding will have implications, of course, but this process is more about understanding than it is about implications. Those will come.

The format is simple: A principle is presented along with some reflections on the principle and some questions. It would be best to stay with a single principle until the group has thoroughly explored its implications for their community.

If these leadership discussions are successful, the same kinds of discussions might then extend into other parish forums, other existing organizations and ministries. There eventually might be small discussion groups formed for ten-week periods just to continue the conversation and to make it available to anyone who is interested. If this happens, additional questions could be written to help the discussions focus on the local parish.

We decided not to include in this booklet any quotes from various documents. Although they would have been helpful in some settings, in others they might have made the material appear too formidable or simply have limited the discussion. However, we encourage those preparing each discussion to search through relevant materials and to bring them to the discussion.

It would be best in any of these settings if all present had copies of this book and the opportunity to read, reflect and make notes beforehand. With that in mind, this book has been designed for active use.

— Gabe Huck

We believe that creation, humanity and human deeds always hold and reveal the presence of God. This sacramental stance is the foundation of our way of living in the world.

The conviction that holiness is found in creation and is found in humanity is the foundation on which the church stands both at prayer and at its daily tasks.

This biblical stance is quite foreign to the dominant power of our age and culture, perhaps more so than to any other time and place. To look on the natural world with eyes formed by the creation story, to approach and respond to our brothers and sisters with habits sharpened by the parables of Jesus, to attend constantly to both evil and good in the doings of humanity — this is the sacramental experience of a Christian life. The alternatives to this way of being are pervasive and powerful.

To sustain and deepen this sacramental way, we have to be nourished with the examples and support of those in our parish community who also strive to live this way. Our way of looking and of living is taken on and held to, little by little, through our bonds to one another.

Make a list of all the ways your parish does what is described here.

Rewrite this principle in a way that sounds like it came out of your own observation of life in your parish. Write it as you would want it said to members of the parish.

Describe experiences in your life that in some way bear out or challenge this principle.

....

....

....

....

....

....

....

....

In this space draw the way you see this principle.

If this principle were music, it would sound a lot like:

....

....

....

What scripture passages does this principle bring to mind?

....

....

....

....

What places in church documents does this principle bring to mind?

....

....

....

....

1. We believe that creation, humanity and human deeds always hold and reveal the presence of God. This sacramental stance is the foundation of our way of living in the world.

Questions

1. How do we as a parish act to show that our human deeds hold the presence of God?

2. In what ways do we accept the diversity of cultural backgrounds, lifestyles and family groupings present in our parish?

3. When do children and youth have opportunities to experience the many ways the church prays?

4. How have those responsible for formal catechesis and those responsible for liturgical celebration (of Sunday eucharist, sacraments, the various rites of the Christian initiation process) established a common outlook, not so much on what should be done in particular celebrations or in catechesis, but on the meaning of sacramental life? How, then, has this been applied to their working together? Have they been able to put into writing the principles that guide their cooperation? Why or why not?

2

3

4

Reflections:

What single direction is most important for our parish? (Answer here and also on page 48.)

2.

The life of a parish is manifest in: attending to God's word, interceding, praising and giving thanks to God, at the Sunday eucharist and in prayer and ritual of many kinds (worship); forming members — young and old, new and veteran — through many ways of teaching (catechesis); building up the body of Christ, the church (community); witnessing to justice and caring for all those in need (service).

This way of sorting out the active life of a parish, based on the Acts of the Apostles, does not divide people by special interests but insists that each member know each of these signs of life. The leadership must struggle with the relationship of these works to each other and to the lives of all who make up the parish.

There are forces that can fragment a parish (e.g., leadership struggles, rigid divisions of activities and responsibilities), and it might be tempting to look to a corporate model to bring efficiency to structure, communications, meetings and other aspects of parish life.

But the corporate world is not a model for the whole of parish life; only scripture can provide that deep and common notion of how all our deeds and needs are bound up and related in this particular community, the body of Christ. Such a gospel image of parish life — not a cliché but a sturdy support on which possibilities can be tested, decisions made and structures set up and evaluated — has to come from the people themselves, including those in leadership positions, pondering and articulating how these tasks (worship, catechesis, community and service) are related and how they are continually done in the parish.

Make a list of all the ways your parish does what is described here.

Rewrite this principle in a way that sounds like it came out of your own observation of life in your parish. Write it as you would want it said to members of the parish.

Describe experiences in your life that in some way bear out or challenge this principle.

In this space draw the way you see this principle.

If this principle were music, it would sound a lot like:

What scripture passages does this principle bring to mind?

What places in church documents does this principle bring to mind?

2. The life of a parish is manifest in: attending to God's word, interceding, praising and giving thanks to God, at the Sunday eucharist and in prayer and ritual of many kinds (worship); forming members — young and old, new and veteran — through many ways of teaching (catechesis); building up the body of Christ, the church (community); witnessing to justice and caring for all those in need (service).

Questions

1. Think about a recent parish activity that you felt particularly good about. What were the things that made it "successful"? What was your goal in planning/participating in the event? How did what you intended to do correspond with what actually happened?

2. How does the integration of the four components (worship, catechesis, community and service) reflect your understanding of the faith life of an active parish?

3. Are there any components of parish life that you would add to these four? Are there any of these four that you would eliminate?

4. How does your parish staff/pastoral team (council) consciously interrelate in the building of community? in the formation of members through prayer and ritual? in catechetical formation? in action for justice?

2

....
....
....
....

3

....
....
....
....

4

....
....
....
....

Reflections:

....
....
....
....
....

What single direction is most important for our parish? (Answer here and also on page 48.)

....
....

3.

Scripture is integral to liturgy and to every aspect of parish life.

The church carries its book and, whenever it is gathered, sings psalms and reads and reflects. Yet scripture remains closed to many Catholics. Good reading and good preaching at the Sunday liturgy and at other gatherings can do much to change this, but more is needed. A parish needs a multitude of ways to engage in lively dialogue with our book. The simplest and perhaps most important way to do this is to bring scripture to the small groups that already exist and to develop new small groups whose primary purpose is simply to grapple regularly with the scriptures, particularly those proclaimed on Sundays. The homily may even emerge from a small group that has reflected on the scriptures with the homilist. Formal religious education should also be thoroughly and deeply biblical.

Make a list of all the ways your parish does what is described here.

Rewrite this principle in a way that sounds like it came out of your own observation of life in your parish. Write it as you would want it said to members of the parish.

....

....

....

....

....

....

....

....

Describe experiences in your life that in some way bear out or challenge this principle.

....

....

....

....

....

....

....

....

In this space draw the way you see this principle.

If this principle were music, it would sound a lot like:

....

....

....

What scripture passages does this principle bring to mind?

....

....

....

....

What places in church documents does this principle bring to mind?

....

....

....

....

3. Scripture is integral to liturgy and to every aspect of parish life.

Questions

1. In what ways does the priority of the Bible make itself felt in all aspects of religious education, especially adult religious education? Are the scriptures integral to catechesis even when catechesis is about an ethical, psychological or institutional topic?

2. In what ways is the lectionary itself understood and applied as it presents a particular reading from one of the gospels or epistles? as it juxtaposes the Hebrew Scriptures with the New Testament? Is there some sense in the parish that such things are not mere "fine points" but are essential because the Bible is essential to us? Why or why not?

3. Who reflects with the homilist prior to the Sunday liturgy? How are the scriptures used as a source for weekly or daily contemplation and action?

4. In what ways do the children of the parish encounter the Bible? What examples do adults give of love for and engagement with the Bible? What examples do the parish staff and leadership give?

2

3

4

Reflections:

What single direction is most important for our parish? (Answer here and also on page 48.)

4. Sacramental life and celebration flourish when all parish ministers, especially those responsible for catechesis and liturgy, work together and share a vision.

Too often we have followed the corporate trends of our times (specialists working independently of one another in education, liturgy, social concerns) and have missed the integrity of Christian life, worship and formation. Catechesis, liturgy, pastoral care and social justice are treated like so many branches of a parent company. Those responsible for these areas share information and schedules, but often they are not working from a common vision. Yet the task of forming Christians can knit their varied tasks into one piece.

All catechesis leads to and flows from participation in the liturgy — for children and adults, for catechumens and others around the order of Christian initiation, for couples at marriage, for parents at the baptism of a child and for whole parishes keeping the liturgical seasons or doing communal anointing. When catechesis sees in the liturgy the rehearsal of our whole lives, it will try to draw all the baptized to embrace the entire ritual life of the church as their right and duty rather than as something they receive or witness. Such participation in the liturgy will, in turn, create a hunger both to learn and to teach. In some members of the church, this hunger is a call to learn the skills of teaching and preaching.

Make a list of all the ways your parish does what is described here.

Rewrite this principle in a way that sounds like it came out of your own observation of life in your parish. Write it as you would want it said to members of the parish.

Describe experiences in your life that in some way bear out or challenge this principle.

In this space draw the way you see this principle.

If this principle were music, it would sound a lot like:

What scripture passages does this principle bring to mind?

What places in church documents does this principle bring to mind?

19

4. Sacramental life and celebration flourish when all parish ministers, especially those responsible for catechesis and liturgy, work together and share a vision.

Questions

1. How does the preparation for and celebration of the sacraments happen in our parish? Who is involved?

2. How are people in different ministries responsible for various aspects of preparation and celebration?

3. How often do the liturgist, catechists, presiders and other ministers meet to reflect, plan and evaluate?

4. How does the parish as a whole experience the efforts of these people?

1

2

3

4

Reflections:

What single direction is most important for our parish? (Answer here and also on page 48.)

5.

Catechesis for all ages takes place within the community in a great variety of settings. In catechesis we are challenged and enabled to ponder, to question and to draw one another on in understanding of and zeal for the gospel.

The ensemble of the church's rites — Sunday word and eucharist, the sacraments, the seasons and feasts of the year, daily prayer — constitutes the first and ongoing formation (and transformation) of all the baptized. In these rituals Catholics become Catholics, becoming ever more a part of a church that ponders and lives by the proclaimed word, that fasts and feasts, that gives alms in many ways, that constantly intercedes and that little by little builds the reign of God, which is glimpsed at liturgy.

But these rites are prepared for and remembered in times of instruction, in catechesis and mystagogia, during which catechumens and faithful ponder everything in light of their rituals. This is true whatever the age or background of the members. In catechesis our Catholic theology, which is itself an evolving reflection on the mysteries of our faith, is studied and discussed. Here we learn where our church has been and take responsible positions about where it will be going; here questions of moral behavior are posed, argued and resolved.

Make a list of all the ways your parish does what is described here.

Rewrite this principle in a way that sounds like it came out of your own observation of life in your parish. Write it as you would want it said to members of the parish.

Describe experiences in your life that in some way bear out or challenge this principle.

In this space draw the way you see this principle.

If this principle were music, it would sound a lot like:

What scripture passages does this principle bring to mind?

What places in church documents does this principle bring to mind?

5. Catechesis for all ages takes place within the community in a great variety of settings. In catechesis we are challenged and enabled to ponder, to question and to draw one another on in understanding of and zeal for the gospel.

Questions

1. How are catechesis and liturgy related in form and in process? How is that expressed in this parish?

2. In what ways does this parish catechize through the church's rites?

3. In this parish, is catechesis subordinated to liturgy, or is liturgy subordinated to catechesis? Explain.

4. How does the parish provide intergenerational sharing of wisdom, prayer, ritual and formation? In what ways have we and do we hand down traditions and rites from one generation to the next?

2

3

4

Reflections:

What single direction is most important for our parish? (Answer here and also on page 48.)

6. Liturgy and catechesis bring the "power of the gospel into the very heart of culture and cultures."

All the dimensions of ritual and the liturgy are done with speech, song, gesture, objects and architecture. Catechesis is done in the language and in the thought and learning patterns of the people. In both liturgy and catechesis, all the human arts in all their cultural expressions are essential. The challenge to local communities of every culture is to celebrate their rites and to do their catechesis in ways that resonate with the gospel itself. Even on the parish level, there needs to be a constant striving to speak in the language and culture of the people, but to speak the gospel.

Make a list of all the ways your parish does what is described here.

Rewrite this principle in a way that sounds like it came out of your own observation of life in your parish. Write it as you would want it said to members of the parish.

....

....

....

....

....

....

....

....

Describe experiences in your life that in some way bear out or challenge this principle.

....

....

....

....

....

....

....

....

In this space draw the way you see this principle.

If this principle were music, it would sound a lot like:

....

....

....

What scripture passages does this principle bring to mind?

....

....

....

....

What places in church documents does this principle bring to mind?

....

....

....

27

6. Liturgy and catechesis bring the "power of the gospel into the very heart of culture and cultures."

Questions

1. Are we as a parish aware of the cultural diversity of our parishioners?

2. Do our rituals (our gestures, actions and music) reflect the great diversity not only of the local church but also of the universal church?

3. How are the cultures, the diversity of lifestyles and the pieties of different cultures shared with the youth of our community?

4. How is our cultural diversity, evident in liturgy and in catechesis, blended with social action in our local community?

2

3

4

Reflections:

What single direction is most important for our parish? (Answer here and also on page 48.)

7.

Sunday eucharist is the central action of parish life. It has a vital relationship to all parish activities and especially to the daily lives of all the baptized.

From both theology and the weekly experience of American parishes we find a compelling reason to recognize that a vital celebration of the Sunday eucharist is essential to all that the parish means and does, as a whole and as groups and individuals. Having recognized this, we then must ask what the criteria are by which the Sunday liturgies are to be judged. What are the ongoing efforts toward the norm of full, conscious and active participation by all the faithful every Sunday? Then we must ask how each area of parish work (e.g., youth ministry, school, religious education, pastoral care, justice ministry) is centered in this Sunday work of the baptized community.

Sunday itself is a ritual for us. We have the cycle of seven days from the Jewish calendar, but the unique character of the first day of the week comes from the New Testament church. Sunday has taken many shapes as Christians have kept it with various practices in different ages and places. Perhaps the name "Lord's Day" expresses its role best: Every day is the Lord's, every day is holy, but for us there must be rhythms to our days. The Sunday rhythm is based first on our gathering, on our assembling for word and eucharist. Should there not be customary ways to prepare for what we do as an assembly? Should there not be ways to keep the hours that follow?

Make a list of all the ways your parish does what is described here.

Rewrite this principle in a way that sounds like it came out of your own observation of life in your parish. Write it as you would want it said to members of the parish.

....
....
....
....
....
....
....
....

Describe experiences in your life that in some way bear out or challenge this principle.

....
....
....
....
....
....
....
....

In this space draw the way you see this principle.

If this principle were music, it would sound a lot like:

....
....
....

What scripture passages does this principle bring to mind?

....
....
....
....

What places in church documents does this principle bring to mind?

....
....
....

7. Sunday eucharist is the central action of parish life. It has a vital relationship to all parish activities and especially to the daily lives of all the baptized.

Questions

1. Little by little, over the years, does it seem that parish members come on Sunday more and more with a sense that they are there to do something? Why or why not? Is that "something" a deed done individually or only as a body?

2. Why should there be customary ways to prepare for what we do as an assembly? Should there be ways for parish members to keep the hours that follow our gathering for word and eucharist? Why? How could this be done?

3. How are the questions and/or concerns of parish members offered for personal reflection and action based on the Sunday readings?

4. What opportunities do the members of the parish (adults, young adults, high school youth, children in catechetical programs, senior citizens, pastoral care workers, and all other groupings) have to reflect on the eucharist (word and sacrifice) and to act from that reflection?

2

3

4

Reflections:

What single direction is most important for our parish? (Answer here and also on page 48.)

8.

The sacraments are the normal actions and celebrations of the assembly, which is all the baptized persons of a parish. The parish itself, then, is the primary symbol because it is the church, the body of Christ, that transacts the sacraments. We believe and we act not as individuals but as the church and even as this church, this parish.

Every time the church gathers, the community manifests in its words and gestures what is holy, what is mystery and what is grace and blessing in the church for the life of the world. These deeds are done by the church, that body of Christ which we are. The special deeds called sacraments, the preparations for their celebration and the mystagogia that follows them are simply a church doing what it needs to do: This whole church initiates, marries, reconciles, anoints, buries, ordains and, above all, gathers on every Lord's Day to do the eucharist.

Make a list of all the ways your parish does what is described here.

Rewrite this principle in a way that sounds like it came out of your own observation of life in your parish. Write it as you would want it said to members of the parish.

Describe experiences in your life that in some way bear out or challenge this principle.

In this space draw the way you see this principle.

If this principle were music, it would sound a lot like:

What scripture passages does this principle bring to mind?

What places in church documents does this principle bring to mind?

8. The sacraments are the normal actions and celebrations of the assembly, which is all the baptized persons of a parish. The parish itself, then, is the primary symbol because it is the church, the body of Christ, that transacts the sacraments. We believe and we act not as individuals but as the church and even as this church, this parish.

Questions

1. How do we celebrate the sacraments communally?

2. How are parishioners informed and catechized about the celebration of the sacraments (baptism of children, communal anointing, reconciliation, confirmation, marriage, orders)?

3. Is the entire assembly invited to celebrations of the sacraments? How and when are they invited to celebrate? How are they invited to participate fully?

4. Do the parish staff and other leaders of the community recognize the importance of celebrating sacraments in the greater assembly of the parish? What hinders such experiences?

2

3

4

Reflections:

What single direction is most important for our parish? (Answer here and also on page 48.)

9. The church's year organizes the sacramental work of the parish.

We see the ordering of the sacramental work of the parish most clearly in the way that the paschal season — from Ash Wednesday to Pentecost — shapes and is shaped by the last steps toward the font and the sacraments of initiation that are celebrated at the Easter Vigil and prolonged through the season of Easter. The church's year creates a rhythm, a repetition that allows the assembly, the baptized people, to exercise their rights and their duties in performing ongoing sacramental deeds. But there are numerous conflicting rhythms in the lives of parishioners and even in the life of the parish itself. The reinvigoration of Lent as a time of both penance and approach to baptism has shown what possibilities there are for a basic, strong rhythm that can deal with the essentials of Catholic life even while we also keep the calendars of our other identities.

Make a list of all the ways your parish does what is described here.

Rewrite this principle in a way that sounds like it came out of your own observation of life in your parish. Write it as you would want it said to members of the parish.

Describe experiences in your life that in some way bear out or challenge this principle.

In this space draw the way you see this principle.

If this principle were music, it would sound a lot like:

What scripture passages does this principle bring to mind?

What places in church documents does this principle bring to mind?

9. The church's year organizes the sacramental work of the parish.

Questions

1. What place do cultural holidays (e.g., Mother's Day) and national holidays (e.g., Thanksgiving) have in the cycle of a parish's life? In what ways does the culture preempt and perhaps distort parts of the Christian tradition?

2. In what ways are the days of Lent, Fridays throughout the year and new, updated ember days occasions for regular encounter with penance and reconciliation in this parish?

3. What does the liturgical year suggest about the baptism of infants? about weddings? about the anointing of the sick? about the way that death is marked in the community? What is the possible future of the feast of All Saints, and All Souls Day? of the whole month of November, which concludes the liturgical year?

4. What other calendars do we operate out of (e.g., the fiscal year and the school year)? How do we catechize about and live out the tension between these calendars and the liturgical year?

2

3

4

Reflections:

What single direction is most important for our parish? (Answer here and also on page 48.)

10.

The celebration of the liturgy, supported by lifelong study, leads to the doing of justice.

Liturgy is not merely an activity parallel to the works of care and justice, to everyday living in kindness and grace, to the willingness to bear one another's burdens. What is the relationship, then, between liturgy and the life of justice? We, the church, in doing the liturgy and our prayers and rituals, are gathered and formed in this foundational love for the world. This is at the heart of our listening to the scriptures, our contemplative habits, our giving thanks and praise on the Lord's Day and every day, our constant intercession and our lamentation and repentance. What is sometimes talked about as the relationship of liturgy to mission or even the relationship of liturgy to life should be understood in this way. Our rituals are not so much about inspiration or consolation or education as they are about the constant expression — to ourselves, to one another and to the Lord — of who we are and who we mean to be: the body of Christ loving this world.

Make a list of all the ways your parish does what is described here.

Rewrite this principle in a way that sounds like it came out of your own observation of life in your parish. Write it as you would want it said to members of the parish.

Describe experiences in your life that in some way bear out or challenge this principle.

In this space draw the way you see this principle.

If this principle were music, it would sound a lot like:

What scripture passages does this principle bring to mind?

What places in church documents does this principle bring to mind?

10. The celebration of the liturgy, supported by lifelong study, leads to the doing of justice.

Questions

1. What acts of social justice does our parish engage in?

2. How are these actions supported by the liturgy and the catechesis of the assembly?

3. What is our parish's effect on the social action of the community?

4. How can we challenge ourselves to act justly, love tenderly and walk humbly with our God? How can we spread this challenge throughout both the leadership and the general population of our assembly?

2

3

4

Reflections:

What single direction is most important for our parish? (Answer here and also on page 48.)

So Where Do We Go From Here?

At the end of a process like this, many people begin to wonder, What do I do now? The most important thing to remember is that you, your staff and all those who are part of the discussion form the "next step."

We do have a few suggestions:

1. Look at what you have written down in this book. Then identify and separate your convictions from your attachments. Convictions are those things you never waver on; they are the ideas that motivate you in your ministry. Attachments are issues and ways of operating that have formed your work in ministry. These, though, can be changed in the interest of the group.

2. Begin to think as a staff: What are we going to do about our present situation? If this book has given you many ideas of different kinds, then look at all of them and spread them over several years. Write down those goals and objectives (there is space to begin this on the final page of this book), and then start looking at them on a regular basis. Where this work affirms your present situation, wonderful! Begin to think of ways that you can reach a larger part of the parish. How can your work in ministry help enlist other people to take part in the mission of the community? If the principles here seem simplistic, then look to the liturgical, catechetical and justice documents for further challenges.

3. Do you think of parish work as collaboration or as collegiality? How would you distinguish them? Collaboration only goes so far. What does collegiality make possible? Does your work bring growth in both each other and the community?

4. Do not turn this book into a "working document" that loses passion. Always go back to the pages where you might have used your "left brain" more. We can't lose poetry, imagery, music and stories. Continue to reflect on the questions that were repeated through this book as your work continues.

5. It was the hope of the original dialogue team that this tool could be used (or refashioned by you) to work in all areas of ministry and in small group gatherings. How could this happen? Could religious educators be in dialogue with liturgists, finance committees with social justice groups, parish councils with Christian initiation teams, and the wisdom generation with the teens of the community? Begin to look at your groups as forming one large circle rather than a top-down structure. Begin to ask the question: CAN WE LIVE THIS DIALOGUE?

6. If you as a group identify specific goals, when will you meet with each other again? There should be formal sessions at which the group discusses whether their goals and objectives are being met, where course corrections are to be made and what principles should be revisited.

There is no single answer in working on "a common sense." The only wrong response would be not to work at all. *Angels in America* put it this way: "We can't stop . . . we are animate . . . even if all we desire is stillness, we still desire. And if we move too fast, so what! What are we waiting for?"

After reading each principle, I want to strive for these things in my ministry:

Principle 1 ....

....

Principle 2 ....

....

Principle 3 ....

....

Principle 4 ....

....

Principle 5 ....

....

Principle 6 ....

....

Principle 7 ....

....

Principle 8 ....

....

Principle 9 ....

....

Principle 10 ....

....

Summary and Directions

The people with whom I originally gathered were:

....

The dates we met were:

....

For each principle, we identified one direction as most important for our parish:

Principle 1 ....

Principle 2 ....

Principle 3 ....

Principle 4 ....

Principle 5 ....

Principle 6 ....

Principle 7 ....

Principle 8 ....

Principle 9 ....

Principle 10 ....

These are the goals and objectives we decided to work on as a team:

....

....

....

These are the general times we are going to check in with each other:

....

....

List here other groups to begin "A Common Sense for Parish Life":

....

....

....